a beauty
only poets can describe

by Ivana Ruzic

Synergy and Light
info@synergyandlight.com

Cover design by: SuziSavanah Hogan
Illustrations by: Katie McGrath
Publicist: Leah Moloney
Typesetting: SuziSavanah Hogan

Published by Synergy and Light
Printed in the United Kingdom 2021

prologue:

oh to be seventeen and in love! such a colossal feeling at such a tender age.

being alone at night made me think about her. how i wished to be in her arms and how i wished we were closer together.

but the issue with me and love is that it consumes me. it was love or it was nothing. everyone says your first love is the hardest to forget, and i think they're right.

love, and especially first love, is the most beautiful thing life has to offer. and i had no idea what i was doing.

throughout this book i am trying to find my way and it's clear it doesn't work because the poems become more and more desperate, and almost every one is a variation of "please don't leave! please don't leave me!"

but my love lives on through this book and i'm proud of it still. because she was a singular beauty that i described and i loved her so.

18/03/20 - 18:46

how can i feel so lonely in a house so full?

how can i feel so lonely in a house so loud?

how can i feel so lonely

surrounded by people

how can i feel so lonely
when i'm not alone at all?

20/03/20 - 23:58

the moon has died.

the moon has died
and i'm looking for the sun.

the darkness isn't as welcoming anymore
it no longer envelops me

it pushes me out
it pushes me away.

i'm looking for the sun
and it's okay

because the sun
is looking for
me too.

21/03/20 - 19:55

your body is a map and i don't think i'd need a compass

23/03/20 - 00:49

i kept a roll of tissue paper in my bedroom
for five months.

i woke up in the mornings
i went to school
i did my homework

but when i went to bed,
when i'd try to go to sleep
i drowned in my own tears.

but then it started getting better
things started getting better.

for some reason it's not enough.

it's not enough right now
and i can't figure out why.

23/03/20 - 01:08

stop
stop!
STOP!

let me press pause!
i am scattered across the cutting room floor!?
let me press pause!

i need a break!
the climax of this movie is going on for too long!??
i need a break!

LET ME PRESS PAUSE
OR I WILL COMBUST

23/03/20 - 01:47

kiss me
please

please just kiss me
i need to feel whole
i need to be held.

i just want to know that someone cares.

i *know* my family cares
i *know* my friends care

but it's not the same.

i want someone to love me.
perfectly

love me
please

please love me.

23/03/20 - 01:52

i have never heard a scream that loud
and when i turned to see who it was,

everyone was looking at *me*?

was it me?
did i crack?

did i finally tell them
to

LOOK AT ME?

i must've
the way they're all staring at me...

27/03/20 - 23:28

your lips are beautiful
i want to feel them on mine

your nose is adorable
especially when you smile

i think you're absolutely gorgeous
all the time.

29/03/20 - 00:29

hi
{please look at me}

how are you
{please look at me}

hey just checking in
{please look at me}

hello it's me again
{please look at me}

where are you
{please look at me}

*{look at me look at me look at me look at me look at me
look at me look at me look at me}*

02/04/20 - 02:23

i feel like
your smile
could make flowers grow

that
your laugh
could make birds sing

10/04/20 - 01:17

the way i'm screaming
LOVE ME LOVE ME LOVE ME

but
i'm not actually screaming

i'm whispering
mumbling

quiet
in the hopes that only you will hear

.

{love me love me love me}

18/04/20 - 02:14

right now
we're on a call
you're asleep
and i'm listening to you breathe
wishing you were next to me

god i wish you were next to me

right now
we're on a call
and you're asleep
i want nothing more than to be in your arms

to feel you against me
to know you're *there*

20/04/20 - 18:02

there's not a moment in time
where you're not on my mind

i think about you when i wake up
i wonder about you during the day
i dream about you when i sleep

you live in my thoughts

i hope you never move out

20/04/20 - 18:40

i want to memorise
the freckles on your body
as if they were my own

i want to trail
my tongue
anywhere i can

so i can taste you

i want to run
my fingers
up and down your thighs

i want to kiss
every part of your body
you don't like

so i can tell you how much i
love it

25/04/20 - 12:50

with your siren call
i am drawn to the sea

drawn to my death
but i don't care because you see me

i love the fact
that you see me

i love that you looked at me and thought;
i want to drive her mad with my song

i can't resist you
i need you
i need to listen to you

even if it's for a split second
i need you to hold me

i can't help myself

25/04/20 - 13:00

the music is pounding
the lights are flashing
we're dancing
and our hands are wandering

i can't stop looking at your lips

you're oblivious
or at least i thought you were

"meet me in the bathroom"

i don't need to look at your lips
because they're all over me
and i can't breathe
i'm not even sure if i can see

all i know right now
is you
your lips
your hands
your *voice*

the music is muffled
the lights are all the same
we're not dancing but i'm in your arms
your hands on my hips and mine in your hair
i can't stop kissing your lips

19

25/04/20 - 16:35

and i woke up in the morning
bleary eyed, head pounding
with kiss stained lips
and bruised hips

where are you?

but i look to my right
and there you are
wrapped up against me
and it feels like home

you feel like home

26/04/20 - 14:09

i tried to write a poem
about how much i hate
that you're always in my dreams

but i don't hate it

i love seeing you there
where everything is perfect
and the lights are low

you have a smile on your face
and your hand is outstretched
waiting for me

the thing i hate

is waking up
right before i reach for you
in my bed

alone

28/04/20 - 16:02

when i look at you
my mouth opens
and instead of speaking
the butterflies that live inside of me
fly out and escape

i smile, suddenly sheepish
but you laugh too
and the more we laugh
the more butterflies
come out
and god it is beautiful

28/04/20 - 17:21

i know they say
don't look at the sun

but how can i not?
when you are so radiant

so bright
and so beautiful

how can i ignore the sun?
when she is right in front of me

telling me that we were meant to be

02/05/20 - 03:01

i am so overcome
with love
that it lives inside of me

it courses through my veins
spelling out your name
and drawing pictures of your face

i am so overcome
with love
that i shout it on the streets

i scream it with pride
that you're the one i get to call mine
and have by my side

i am so overcome with love

04/05/20 - 01:28

every day
i wake up
wanting to see you
and to tell you
how much i love your hair
or your eyes
or your lips
or your nose
or you in general
because i love everything about you

04/05/20 - 22:32

today i lay on the ground
and watched the sky
and it was sad
because i wished you were by my side
so i could look
and see you in the corner of my eye
and maybe hold your hand

while we watched the sky

together

04/05/20 - 22:36

i'm talking about the sky again
because i wondered
what you were doing then
were you looking at it too?
was it like mine?
clear blue?

is it cliché to say
that it reminded me of your eyes?
that i wished i was looking at them?

please tell me
what you were doing today
when i was looking at the sky
and thinking of you

07/05/20 - 19:27

i want to spend
a day in bed with you
i want to wake up to you
and i want to be in your arms
for hours
i want to whisper
a million
i love yous
while you fall asleep
i want to wake you
in the middle of the night
to ask for a kiss
i want to listen to music
while the sun sets
i want to lay my head
on your chest
to hear your heartbeat
and compare it to mine

i want to spend a day in bed
with you

07/05/20 - 19:38

i love
how you turn my mind to mush
i love
how the thought of you makes me smile
i love
how talking to you makes it easier to sleep
i love
how your words have such a strong effect on me

i love
thinking about the memories we're going to make
i love
thinking about how your voice sounds
i love
thinking about your smile
i love
thinking about the fact that i am yours and you are mine

13/05/20 - 16:05

you know when you're in a pool
and you put your head under the water
and everything goes quiet

that's how you make me feel

i'm drowning in the best way possible
i cannot breathe
but it's okay because you are all i see

17/05/20 - 21:39

tonight i looked at my blinking fairy lights
and they weren't the stars
but i wished they were

i was looking at them and thinking of you

they weren't the stars
but i wished you were looking at them too

i wished you were here with me
looking at the 'stars'
where i'd be safe in your arms

19/05/20 - 22:19

let me rip open my chest
hands clawed and blood pouring

let my heart pump
let me show you it beating

the way it beats for you

take away my ribcage
it's blocking the view

look at my lungs
watch them stop as i look at you

you leave me breathless

21/05/20 - 05:10

i'm listening to the birds right now

i wish i was listening to you breathe

21/05/20 - 13:52

i want to learn every mundane thing about you.

are you a morning person or a night owl? when you're
brushing your teeth do you wet your toothbrush and then
put the toothpaste on or do you do it the other way around?
what's your favourite piece of clothing? what did you want
to be when you were younger? what's your comfort food?
what's the best song to cry to, in your opinion? what books
did you love as a child? how do you like your tea and coffee?

please tell me all the 'boring' things about you because i am
dying to know.

22/05/20 - 21:17

i feel as though
we are two different flowers
in the same field

26/05/20 - 00:09

your past does not define you
and it is not my place to judge

what matters to me
is here
and now
and what will be

02/06/20 - 00:59

i don't know
how to keep my feelings to a minimum
it's all or nothing

i love you with my heart and soul
or not at all

i'm blasé and unaffected
or i'm inconsolable and heartbroken

for me
there is only two ends of the spectrum

and i feel too much
or not at all

i wish i felt nothing at all more often

05/06/20 - 17:27

and the weather is very cold right now
and i'm wishing you were here
holding me in your arms
my warm breath against your neck
your hand tracing patterns on my back

please hold me
i am aching for your touch
i need it
i need you

oh god i am aching for your touch

06/06/20 - 00:40

i feel like you're not real
like you're a figment of my imagination

someone i've made up
to say all the right things
and look the right way

someone i've made up
to write about
and to think about

i need you to be real
please please please
please be real

06/06/20 - 00:48

i try, you know
to get you off my mind
to think about something
anything else

don't get me wrong
i love thinking about you
i love you
but i'm so scared

it's like you consume me
everything i do
leads me back to you
it's disorienting

what will i do
if you go
what will i think about
what will consume me then?

what will consume me then?

09/06/20 - 00:58

i always read poems
about talking to the moon
but for me
it's not just the moon
it's the sun
it's the stars
it's the plants by my window
it's my dog
it's the posters in my room

i'll talk to anything
just to talk about you

11/06/20 - 02:13

i tied a rock to my shoe
to keep me grounded

but the balloon on my wrist
just lifted me higher and higher

and really how could i resist
being up in the air

the sky is so blue
and the sun is so bright

what's the point of staying on the ground
when i can just as easily have my head in the clouds

13/06/20 - 01:57

i'd rather live in the dreams
i've made up
where everything is perfect
and the weather is good
than to return to my bed
where i can hear the rain
and my feet are too cold

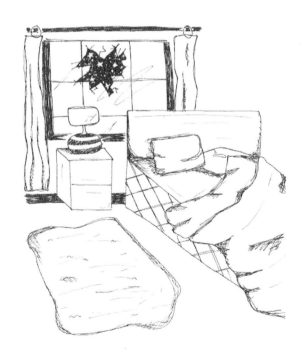

18/06/20 - 02:52

i wish

that when you looked in the mirror
you'd see yourself through my eyes

that the thoughts in your brain
were actually things i'd say

20/06/20 - 14:47

and like a child
asking for something sweet

i looked at you
and begged for love

i prodded
i pestered
i cried

i begged

21/06/20 - 02:29

i wonder
sometimes
if i am real
i look down
and my hands are there
they move
i look at my feet
my painted toes

but then i begin to fade away
like dust i've just blown off the table
i just
disappear
i am not here
not really
in my mind
god in my mind

i am in your arms and it is warm
it is soft
in my mind
when i look down
i don't see myself lying in my bed
we are

we are on a cloud
and there's nobody else

i wonder
sometimes
if i am real
and i am
but not in the way i want to be
i am alone
and that's the worst of it all
i belong on a cloud with you

but i am alone

02/07/20 - 00:23

when i'm with you
time seems to stop
and speed up
simultaneously

because when i see you
at two in the afternoon
the world stops
and it's just us

but then i look at the clock
and suddenly it's two in the morning
and i want nothing more
than to stay in your arms

for another 24 hours

07/07/20 - 23:59

you left my body
decomposing in my bed
the taste of your lips
still on my skin

08/07/20 - 00:04

you pick at my petals
crying
"she loves me"
"she loves me not"

i love you!!!!
i do!!!
stop pulling me apart!!
stop ripping my skin to shreds!

13/07/20 - 00:46

if i stripped my body bare
left myself as a bundle of nerves
and exposed muscles

would you love me then?

if you could choose how i looked
and how i sounded
what i wore

would you love me then?

if i wasn't me at all
my brain detached
just a body

would you love me then?

16/07/20 - 00:14

if i could
extract myself
from the mirror
and fall in love with her
i would

she wouldn't hurt me
i don't think
i am her
she is me

what's the point?

but maybe she will
maybe she'll realise
how annoying i am
maybe she'll see
what everyone else sees

if i were in a relationship
with myself
would i still love her
would i notice
the things that get on her nerves?

16/07/20 - 00:44

my teeth are falling out
the house is on fire
the kids are playing outside

i'd quite like
to wrap myself up in my blankets
lie in bed

and burn

kill me
along with the house
perhaps i won't feel so alone

so lonely

i love my bed
it knows me better than anyone
the stories i've told and the places i've seen

my teeth are gone so take my tongue
my vocal cords too
so i can't scream,

burn me with my bed
with my house
while the kids are playing outside

16/07/20 - 00:52

i'm not a child
i'm not a child
i'm not a child

i'm a bomb
a ticking one
time is running out!

run away!
be safe!
because i will blow up!

i'll be worse than anything before

see no one knew about the bomb
didn't know where it was

i kept it a secret
obviously
wouldn't want to raise suspicion

i needed everything to be perfect you see
well surprise! i'm telling you now!
time is running out!

run away!
be safe!

16/07/20 - 00:59

i dragged the knife
down my stomach
just to see what was inside
were the butterflies really there?

will i find a dead one?

will i find a dozen?

don't they look beautiful!
such a dark, rich red
i might have to frame them
i can't believe the butterflies were there!

would you like one?
you can have it
you can have them all
they're yours

you made them didn't you?
that *was* you, right?

17/07/20 - 23:35

i'm sorry i was scared
can i kiss you again?
i wanted to be perfect
please can i kiss you again?
i won't be afraid this time
i'm begging you
come over soon
let me kiss you
i know what to do now

please

can i kiss you again?

28/07/20 - 01:09

"look up"

and when i did
you were there
and christ
it was like seeing the entire world
right in front of me

you grabbed my hand
and i swear i felt
the branches and vines
cuffing our wrists together
and they kept growing and growing
until they were all around us

and i looked up
and you were everywhere
oh how i love looking up at you
how i love when you're all i see
how i love when you look down at me
oh god how i love

28/07/20 - 01:39

suddenly
my mind is in my toes
and there are words running
all through my body
but none come together to describe you
or how i feel about you
or how you make me feel

it's as though
the words are there
but they're in a different language
i can't make sense of them
they don't make sense
my mind is in my toes
it's like frostbite
my feet are numb

29/07/20 - 19:02

sometimes i think
the reason i care so much
about love
is because to me
it's a representation
of all that is good
in the world

if i'm focused on love
and being in it
and the thought of it
i can avoid
my worries
my insecurities
and the things that make me stressed

when i am in love i am fine
because it is all that exists to me
everything else is swept under the rug
i don't need it
i don't need to worry about it
because i am in love
and that is what matters

29/07/20 - 19:07

i don't believe in god
but if it means keeping you in my life
i will pray to him every night
and beg at the hands of the church
to stop you from leaving

i'll bathe in holy water
i'll gorge myself on sacramental bread
i'll choke on their wine

please don't leave
please don't leave
please don't leave me

i am begging
i'm begging and i'm praying and i'm hoping
i need you to stay
i need you

i need you!

I NEED YOU!

01/08/20 - 00:55

i took your laugh
i put it in my pocket

and throughout the day
i put my hand in

just to hear it reverberate
against my palm

it was your laugh
but it belonged to me

mine
it happened when we were together

i love your laugh
i love listening to it

even if it was at my expense
i still love your laugh

04/08/20 - 22:39

the thought of you
kissing someone else
someone that isn't me

it brings a feeling
that i can't quite describe
it breaks me

to think of you
holding someone else
someone that isn't me

god how do i even begin to explain
that it absolutely rips me to shreds
to think about

i try not to
i try not to think about it
but i am terrified

i'm so utterly scared
that you will find someone
better, someone prettier, lovelier

the thought of you
with someone else
someone that isn't me
is scary

interlude

i have spent my life waiting to be loved. waiting for this love to complete me.

but the problem was never an inability to be loved. it was my ache, my terrible need for this love.

having this love upheaved all of these insecurities. it turned my vision inwards, watching the desperate part of myself begging for love, looking for it in every crevice of the earth.

i needed the love to consume me.

i needed it to embrace me.

04/08/20 - 23:27

i feel so empty
and i try to fill the gaps
i try so hard
to fill them with love
but it's like there's something wrong
i don't know what it is

i feel so empty
i don't know what to do
i don't want to be here
please help
i'm trying and it's so difficult
i just want some help

i feel so empty
and i am looking for others
to fill these gaping holes in my soul
but nothing is working
that void is still there
i need to fill the hole myself

05/08/20 - 00:30

i asked my mother to draw me
and the picture i got back
was a little girl
with wide eyes
and a bright smile
and hair down to her ankles

but that is not me

the image of me
in my mother's head
is not me
i don't look like that little girl
and i don't act like her
sometimes i wish i did

that is not me

05/08/20 - 00:47

i am rotting

i am rotting i am rotting i am rotting

god look at my corpse
it's disgusting

eyes open
mouth wide
jaw unhinged
skin green

i am disgusting
grotesque
i am rotten

i just saw a fly
come out of my mouth

i'm a walking corpse

06/08/20 - 00:08

i bought a venus flytrap today
i fed it a fly
now i wish
it devoured me instead
i wish i was clenched
between its jaws
that it was digesting *me*
for a week
instead of the fly
i wish that next Wednesday
i will have stopped existing

06/08/20 - 00:59

it rained today
so i went outside
i lay on the grass

it was like drumming
all around me
steady, peaceful

with every beat and thud
i sank deeper and deeper
into the mud

until it was in my mouth
and in my nose
until it covered my eyes

i was sinking
and i didn't care

i just wanted to drown

end interlude

10/08/20 - 23:31

i'd want to see you
in heaven
or in hell
or at the supermarket

i'd want to see you
when i'm young
and energetic
and loud

i'd want to see you
when i'm old
and tired
and spent

there is no time
no time at all
where you're not on my mind
i'd want to see you, always

11/08/20 - 00:22

can everyone
please
get out of my head
the door is right there

please
can you just get out
i don't want to think
not anymore

i don't want you to think for me
get out of my head
let me think for myself
please

why is everyone
clogging up my brain
there's too many people here
get out

god i am begging you
please just get
out
of
my
head

                                        even you my love.

11/08/20 - 01:48

i wanted to tell you something
to tell you that i'd kiss
every last one of your insecurities
until you believed
that they were beautiful

i wanted to tell you
so i turned to the right
and you weren't there
and i looked up
but you weren't there

you're not there
and all i want
is to tell you that i think
you're so utterly beautiful
that it baffles me

but you're not there

20/08/20 - 00:41

what am i
who am i
if not yours

what do i think
what do i feel
if not feelings for you

what do i watch
where do i look
if not your ineffable face

what do i touch
what do i actually *feel*
if not your warm calloused hands

what do i taste if not your lips
what do i smell if not your dizzying perfume

what do i do if my world isn't revolving around you

where do i go
what do i say
if not what i need you to hear

i am yours
now tomorrow and forever
i am always yours

25/08/20 - 01:42

i want to write you a book
to tell you how i feel
i want to watch you read it
and see your smile grow
and have you look at me
and grab my hand
to tell me
"thank you.
i love this.
i love you."
because i love you too
i do
i need you to know
but you do
oh you do

25/08/20 - 01:46

i listen to music
and you're in the lyrics
so i turn it off

i listen to the rain
but you're in the wind
so i turn on the tv

i watch the movie
and you're in every character
so i pick up a book

i read the pages
and every word reminds me of you
so i lift my pen

i write about you
and you're in all my poems
so i write more

and more

and more

25/08/20 - 01:55

i died in the woods
wearing my white dress
oh sure it's dirty now
with animals crawling all over it
and there are roots growing through my eye sockets
and flowers sprouting from my mouth

but tell me

is that not
just as lovely
just as beautiful
just as poetic

as when i wore my white dress first?

when the trees grew around us
and carved our path
when i was holding your hand
and watching you laugh
when i was making you smile
and calling you mine

25/08/20 - 02:12

i love sleeping
i love escaping
people
life
myself

when i'm asleep
i dream
and it's so sweet
i dream of you
oh it's perfect
i dream of us
and oh god it's everything i want
i dream of you and me

i want you you you
in my head it's all about you
i miss you during the day when i'm awake
i miss you at night when i'm asleep
i want to scream
i want to
tear
myself
apart
and shout

i want you you you
everything is about you you you

are you okay? do you need a hug?
do you need to cry?
the dream is perfect
reality sad and depressing

i don't care about anything but you

25/08/20 - 02:39

i sometimes wish
people could read my mind
so they'd know how i felt
and they wouldn't say anything
but they'd know
and i wouldn't have to tell them
and it'd be perfect
because they'd look at me and *know*
and my voice wouldn't crack
and there'd be no lump in my throat
just them looking at me
and knowing

25/08/20 - 02:58

i read something
and it asked
"when you think of love
do you think of pain?"

and my answer to that is no
i don't think of pain
i think of you
it's always you

i think of the first time we spoke
and the first time i saw you
i think of your smile
and your hair (i love your hair)

and it's not painful
because you make me happy
extremely so
you're perfect in your own little way

                                        perfect to me

                                        perfect for me

25/08/20 - 04:04

rip my tongue out and call it a kiss
slit my wrists and call it love
saw my arms off and call it a hug

watch me bleed and call it romance

30/08/20 - 00:26

so i scream about love
and i cry about love
and my world revolves around love
and it's love love love
and i don't care
because it's all that matters
and without it i'd be nothing

it is at the centre of my universe

and i say 'it' when i mean you
because love to me is loving you
you are love
you are my love
and i don't care
because you're all that matters

without you
i am nothing

02/09/20 - 02:05

i would count
all the stars in the sky
a thousand times over
just to hold your hand again

i would rip
every blade of grass
from my garden
just to kiss you again

i would separate
every strand of hair
on your head
just to hear you say "i love you" again

and maybe i deserve the world
i do
but you deserve it more
and i want to give it to you
i want to give you the entire universe
please take it
i am giving it to you

please
take me
i am giving
myself to you

08/09/20 - 15:22

i had a dream last night
and you were in my room
lying on your stomach
and i lay on you
and i kissed your neck and i kissed all the way
from your left fingertips
across your shoulder blades
down to your right thumb
and i kissed every spot on your back
that i could reach
down to the bottom of your spine
and then i lay down beside you
and i watched you close your eyes
i watched you smile
and suddenly i was smiling too

you know you're beautiful, don't you?

11/09/20 - 00:57

i feel very soft
and i feel very fragile
if you held me
i'm afraid i'd break
if you grabbed my hand
or hugged me close
i'm not sure
my bones would survive
i'm not sure
i would survive

13/09/20 - 00:34

i feel like a walking corpse
my eyes are sunken
my teeth are rotting
my skin is cracking
my bones are breaking
my body is failing
and i am so very fragile
one touch and i'd disintegrate

15/09/20 - 17:08

i want to be the air you breathe
so i can be close to you
and get inside your body
and see all that you're made of
i'd love to get inside of you
and plant little kisses along your lungs
and show the butterflies
where to flutter inside your stomach

i want to be the air you breathe
so i can be near to you
and get inside your body
and see the things that make you hurt
i'd love to get inside of you
and go to your brain
and see what's on your mind
so i can place the thought of me inside

i want to be the air you breathe

please think about me

23/09/20 - 00:04

i wanted to write the phrase
a thousand times over
"a beauty only poets can describe"
i wanted to hear you say it
a thousand times over

i am a poet
i am a poet
i am a poet

oh please
let me describe you
it's all i want to do
it's all i want to write
your beauty only i can describe

i want to hear you say it to me
"a beauty only poets can describe"
i heard it and it played on repeat
inside my head
it's you, it's your name, it's all that you are

the words float around my brain
with images of you at the core
you are the word beauty personified
you are indescribable
you are inexplicable

23/09/20 - 00:41

i look around
and you're not there
so i close my eyes
and you're right beside me
and so i keep them closed
as long as possible
i sleep
for as long as possible
because you're right beside me
and i am holding your hand
listening to your laugh
i am closing my eyes

but they're open
they're open all the time
and it's exhausting
because really all i want
is to see you
i need my eyes to close
i need them closed
and if i do it right now
i can feel you beside me
your hand around me
your hands *on* me

i close my eyes
and there you are

27/09/20 - 01:16

sometimes
i have visions
of grabbing my face
from either side

and pulling

the skin rips
and the blood pours
and i'm about to see what's underneath
about to see who i really am

but the thought stops there

until it starts again
and i am shredding my skin
and it is a blood bath
i am ripping myself apart

but who am i
who am i!?
who the hell am i?!

WHO AM I?

02/10/20 - 00:36

i am not me
i am not whole
there is pieces of everyone
and every story i've told
i lose a part of myself
whenever i lose a person
and it's so frustrating
because all i want to be
is me

05/10/20 - 14:46

you're a calamity
please get inside of me
get as close as you can possibly be
you're a catastrophe
maybe we're meant to be
love is a tragedy
(get inside of me)
i need you near, can't you see?
you're a calamity
a calamity
a calamity

08/10/20 - 13:08

i'm sorry
if i bothered you
last Thursday
asking for constant kisses
i was scared
that i wouldn't be able to do it again
and you know me and time

always scared it'll run out
always scared it'll run away

i think i take the phrase
"live each day as if it were your last"
too literally
because i feel as though
i won't be alive tomorrow
and i panic
i'm always panicking

i want to get it all done
i want to see it all before i die

09/10/20 - 22:55

i'm going to gouge out my eyes
right from my skull

nothing's working
i need them closed
i need them shut

anything to stop seeing
fuck!
why can't i close my eyes

i'm so tired
the bags under them are heavy
please

i just want to close my eyes

18/10/20 - 12:26

i don't want to live
if i have to live without you

it sounds dramatic
and it is i know it is

i can feel you slipping through my fingers

and it's making me scream
it's making me cry

please stay

please stay

i can't let you go
i don't want to let you go

you're all i have
you're all i need

please stay

please,

stay

18/10/20 - 12:41

i want to be enough
i feel like i'm never enough

i feel like they always want more
either from me
or someone else entirely

and i'm good
but i'm not good enough

i just want someone to look at me
with stars in their eyes
and love in their heart

i want them to think about *me*
and just me not someone else

i want to be enough
i just want to be enough

22/10/20 - 01:39

so i'm left with thoughts of you
that you don't want to hear
thoughts that still have my stomach
doing flips and tricks
thoughts of you in my bed
in my arms
thoughts of your smile
and your laugh

and i can't just turn my brain off

i can't just forget about you

so i think and think and think
and it's mental torture
because i miss the feel of your skin

22/10/20 - 03:14

how do i tell you i love you
without telling you

how do i tell you i *need* you

there's moments in the day
where i feel like something is missing
i feel like a part of me is missing

and baby i know it's you

you've stolen not just a piece of my heart
but the entire organ

it is yours entirely

to play with
to break

i am yours entirely

to play with
to break

25/10/20 - 01:43

i want a love that's like star gazing at 3am
i want a love that's like waking up and getting
a kiss on the head
i want a love that completes me
i want a love that fills the empty spaces of my heart
i want a love that consumes me
i want to be consumed

25/10/20 - 22:34

it's raining tonight
and i'm staring at the ceiling
and i'm thinking of how you're feeling
have you been sleeping?
i know we haven't been speaking

i'll give you my love
i'm not sure you need it
but maybe it can help
maybe it'll ease your pain
maybe you'll sleep again

and if there's ever a day
where i can never see your face
i pray that someone
leaves and takes my eyes out on the way
because if i can't see you my love
nothing i look at will ever be enough

29/10/20 - 12:05

i can't help seeing you in a holy light
as in
i am on my knees
and my hands are at your feet
and you are god
my god
and my love is my religion
my bible is my poems
my communion is your kiss

05/11/20 - 00:22

i'm very cold right now
i'm wondering if you're thinking the same

remember when
i told you my room was warm
you didn't believe me
but do you remember
how i felt in your arms?
do you remember
looking down at me?
tell me please
i miss kissing you
i miss the feel of your skin
it's unbearably soft

i love you

05/11/20 - 01:26

you are the breath in my lungs
and you are the sun on my skin
you are the blood in my veins
you are the start of every day
and you are the end of every night
you are *it*

there's nobody like you
there will be nobody like you

05/11/10 - 03:08

3am i've got you on my mind again
but to be honest you never really left

"you mean to tell me
you think of nothing else?"

no
i don't
you are in the back of my mind 24/7
and it's infuriating
but i also don't mind all that much
i like you being there
i like knowing you're there

14/11/20 - 00:21

i had a lot of feelings
i have a lot of feelings
but lately
for whatever reason
i feel very empty inside
hollow almost
i just don't care
i don't care anymore
it's like it doesn't matter
nothing matters these days
and i don't know what's going on
but i want to care again
i don't like feeling empty
usually it's my stomach
but now it's my brain
my entire being
there's nothing inside
there's no drive
i am a shell
i'm an empty home

i feel as if i'm all alone

                                        am i alone?
                                   do you love me?

author's note + acknowledgements:

i get a lot of people asking me for advice on writing poetry, but the truth is i don't know how i do it. honestly, i have spent sleepless nights thinking about nothing other than my feelings. and of course, most people have normal sleep schedules, so i couldn't really talk to anyone about these feelings. which is where the notes app on my phone came in very handy!

when i don't quite know how to articulate my feelings, i find it much easier to do so under the veil of poetry. it allows me to "make my feelings pretty" for lack of a better phrase. for me, poetry is my way of baring my soul to the world without ever saying a word. sometimes, i like to imagine that i am only writing my poetry for one person, who is so often referred to as "you" throughout the book.

in all honesty this book would not have been possible without SuziSavanah, who walked me through the entire process with the utmost patience, and allowed me to create something that is completely my own.

my best friend Katie also had a colossal role for this book, in which she drew me a multitude of truly beautiful images to go with my poems. i'd be lost without her by my side all these years.

i'd also like to thank my family, who continue to love and support me through my writing endeavours, especially my mother, who has almost always taught me to stay true to myself, no matter what.

and finally to you. my beauty, my muse, my first love. this book wouldn't even have been written in the first place if it wasn't for you. you are my best friend. every day i am grateful that you came into my life. thank you for teaching me so much about myself. you will always hold a piece of my heart, and i do quite love you.

- Ivana <3

Synergy and Light is an independent publisher, based in Ireland, dedicated to stories. Stories of life, of death, of myth, of legend. Stories from authentic voices and people who have a precious gem to share with the world. If this sounds like you, and you have a completed, edited first draft, please reach out and email us at info@synergyandlight.com. Perhaps we can work our magic and make the synergy and light of your creativity flow out into the world!

Many Blessings,

SuziSavanah x

Printed in Great Britain
by Amazon